The Red Kite in Wales

THE RED KITE IN WALES

John Evans

CHRISTOPHER DAVIES

First published by Christopher Davies (Publishers) Ltd.
P.O. Box 403, Sketty,
Swansea, SA2 9BE.

ISBN 0 7154 07112

Set in New Century Schoolbook by
Words, Swansea
Printed by
Dinefwr Printing Company,
Llandybie, Dyfed.

Kite in a Gale

Kite uses the wind
as a dancer uses her muscular partner,
subservient, there to throw and lift her,
all his violence planned, harmless,
his capitulation certain.

Kite, fork-tail spread, glides
balancing, steady on a gust
that rips off new-leaved branches;
then at her will tilts down the wind
and is gone, blown away sideways
with the spring leaves that had no choice.

Ruth Bidgood

Contents

The Red Kite

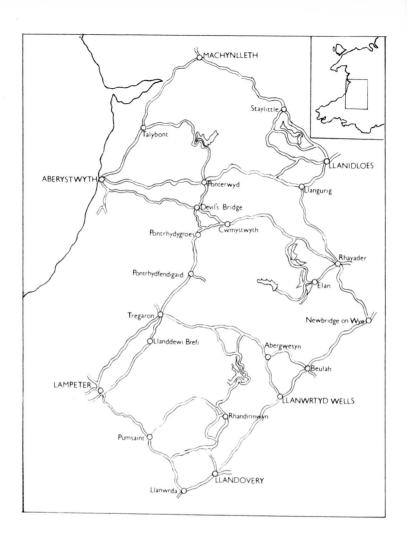

Preface

The red kite, now amongst the rarest of our breeding birds, was up until about the eighteenth century the most familiar bird of prey in this country. Even the City of London could boast an abundance of kites which were frequently sighted feeding on the open drains and sewers in the city. However, with the cleaning up of our towns and cities, the destruction of natural habitats, and the savage persecution of the bird in rural areas by gamekeepers and misguided farmers, by the year 1900, its numbers were so reduced that only three pairs remained. These few remaining birds had somehow managed to survive in the remote upland valleys of central Wales, where they held on precariously to their existence until a group of conservationists finally decided to stand up in their defence. Thankfully, due by and large to the endeavours of these people, with their careful watches to guard against would-be egg collectors and their gradual persuasion of local hill farmers that the kite presented no real threat to their livelihoods, the bird was brought back from the very edge of extinction in this country, and has, since those early days, made a slow and sometimes painful increase in numbers to about 47 pairs today.

Of course the fight for the preservation of the kite is still carried on today, through the activities of the RSPB as well as many of the other organizations for conservation in this country, and though there are some signs of further increases and more widespread dispersal of the bird's numbers, the red kite is still only found in Wales, remaining faithful to those same upland valleys that so enabled its survival in those traumatic years at the beginning of the century.

In this book, I have tried to answer most of the questions that surround the bird, in the hope that given a better understanding, people will never again allow such a dreadful fate to befall this large and handsome hawk. I have also included a chapter in the book which I hope will serve both as a guide to those who visit the area specifically to see the red kite, as well as being a source of information to those wishing to explore some of the many other attractions that exist in this very beautiful part of Wales.

John Evans

The Red Kite in Wales

1. The Natural History of the Red Kite

Although it seems difficult to believe now, at one time the kite was perhaps the most familiar bird of prey in Great Britain, breeding throughout England, Wales and Scotland (only ever a rare vagrant in Ireland).

In London in particular, it was a very common sight, so much so that "foreigners were struck with its abundance".[1] One visitor to England in 1461, declared "that he had nowhere seen so many kites as around London Bridge",[2] and in 1555, Belon observed that "they were scarcely more numerous in Cairo than in London".[3] Shakespeare himself described London as a "city of kites and crows".[4] It is doubtful if the bird was in quite such an abundance in other parts of the country, for like its relative the black kite, it tends to congregate where garbage is most plentiful,[5] and the open drains, and the refuse on the streets and on the Thames were a major attraction to the bird. Indeed it was such a useful scavenger that it was protected by the law of the city for its value in keeping the streets clean.

However, this attitude towards the bird did not exist in rural areas. There it was regarded as a troublesome pest and rewards were paid for its destruction, and when later, game protection came to the fore, the birds' fate was finally sealed. "The gamekeepers armed with new and more effective weapons, exterminated the bird most effectively."[6]

This intolerance to the bird, somehow must have spread to the city, for by the end of the eighteenth

century the red kite had lost its protected status in the City of London.

By 1734 some kites still nested in the trees around St Giles-in-the-Fields, but by 1777 comes the last recorded nesting of the bird in London. The story of the kite in London draws to a close with one seen flying over Piccadilly on 24 June 1859.

Of course the fate of the bird was similar throughout the country, with much persecution of this chicken-snatching thief taking place during the breeding season, and many of the birds killed for reward were young taken from the nest. By the beginning of the nineteenth century the kite had disappeared without trace from the records of half the counties of England, and this was soon to be repeated elsewhere.

The last breeding kites disappeared from Yorkshire early in the century, from Kent in 1815, and from Berkshire, Oxfordshire, Cambridgeshire, Norfolk, Suffolk and Northumberland in around 1830. They nested for the last time in Huntingdonshire in 1837, and in Rutland and Cumberland in 1840. They held out in Northamptonshire until 1845, Worcestershire to 1850, and Essex until about 1855, and the last breeding kites in England were exterminated in Lincolnshire in 1870 (although one pair nested in Devonshire in 1913, and another in Cornwall in 1920).

This all too familiar pattern was repeated in Scotland (the last pair nested in Perthshire in 1880) causing E.V. Baxter and L.J. Rintoul to remark in their book *The Birds of Scotland*, that "the principal feature of the disappearance of the kite in Scotland was the rapidity with which this was affected".[7]

This sudden disappearance of the kite from Scotland, as well as other parts of the country, would seem to suggest that the weather must have played its part in the extermination of the bird. For only something such as a severe winter could have brought about a disappearance of such extreme rapidity, and in the cases of most forms of persecution of the kite (shooting, trapping etc.) the decrease in numbers would surely have been more gradual.

One other factor not as yet mentioned, which might have played some small part in diminishing the numbers of the kite population, was its pursuit by trained falcons. For in the early days of falconry, the kite was looked upon as a supreme prize, and there are many accounts of the bird being killed for sport.

Whatever the reason or reasons were that brought about such a decimation of the birds' population, by the year 1900 there were only three pairs left, chancing to survive in the remote upper Tywi valley of central Wales. (In Wales itself the kite had at one time been common, but had undergone the same extreme decrease in numbers as in other parts of the country. Even the now industrialised valleys of south Wales, could show on their once thickly wooded slopes, kites and buzzards breeding alongside herons and rooks.) Indeed if it had not been for the endeavours of the British Ornithologists Club, the species would undoubtedly have been exterminated from these shores. Some members of the club even set up a fund for the preservation of the kite in Wales,[8] and many others assisted actively with their support.

Between the years 1900 to 1907, there was an average of only three pairs. There was a gradual increase to about ten pairs between 1912 and 1920, but by 1921 the numbers had slumped dramatically, dropping to three breeding pairs that year. In 1927 this number had more than doubled, and in the same year an attempt was made by Mr C.H. Gowland to restock the British kite population, by bringing in fresh blood from overseas. He imported 21 eggs of Spanish kites. These were placed in the nests of buzzards in central Wales, in the hope that the buzzards would bring up the kites as their own. However, it was far from successful, and only two hatched. In the following year another attempt was made. Fifty-three eggs were imported and placed in buzzards' nests, this time with far better results as 31 hatched, the buzzards proving themselves to be good foster parents. Despite this success, apart from some young birds seen in central Wales the following year, the kite population was not greatly increased as expected. The failure of this experiment seems to to be due to the fact that the Spanish kite is migratory (unlike our own bird) hence the young dispersed never to return.

Over the next 20 years the population was subject to the same fluctuations as at the beginning of the century, with only four pairs breeding successfully between the years 1933 and 1937, five pairs in 1938 and 1939, and again only four pairs breeding successfully in 1945. The eggs of the bird had now become increasingly more valuable to collectors, and as more and more attempts were made at stealing the eggs, the conservationists were forced to be far more vigilant, with local watches responsible for each

Irfon Valley

Dinas Bird Reserve (R.S.P.B.)

nest. In 1937, Miss Dorothy Raikes took charge of the kite preservation fund, which as a body worked hard to preserve the few know breeding areas.

From 1950 onwards, there was a marked improvement in the fortunes of the red kite in this country. As a result of both the strengthening of the laws for wildlife conservation and a reduction in the use of illegal poisons in agricultural practices, numbers were allowed to increase significantly, rising to 15 pairs in 1962, 21 pairs in 1969, and 34 pairs in 1976. In more recent years, happily this trend has continued and there were 48 breeding pairs in 1986.

The years 1987 and 1988 saw a further development in the fight for the preservation of the kite. It was decided jointly by the Royal Society for the Protection of Birds and the Nature Conservancy Council, that because of the bird's poor success rate when breeding, a programme of artificial rearing of wild kite eggs should be undertaken. The eggs from some of the more vulnerable nest sites were removed soon after laying and substituted with dummy eggs. The eggs were then hatched in incubators or by bantam hens, and the young chicks returned to the nests in the wild. Despite some setbacks to the programme (infertility of the eggs etc.) in 1987 from the 13 eggs removed, five young birds were successfully returned to the wild, and in 1988, there was a slight improvement with eight young chicks returned to the wild out of the ten eggs removed that year.

As the population has increased, so the birds are spreading farther afield, which can only be good for their long-term development, but at this still crucial stage, it is an added burden on those seeking to protect them, as they now have to cover a far greater area to make sure the birds are well protected wherever they choose to breed.

Let us hope now, in these more enlightened times that there will be a far more responsible attitude towards the birds from the general public, gamekeepers, farmers etc. in making sure that this slow but steady increase in the birds' numbers is not hindered, and we never again return to the situation as it was at the beginning of the century.

Devil's Bridge

2. Why Wales?

Why when the red kite was subject to such fierce persecution, as to almost bring about its extinction from these shores, did it manage to survive in the rainy hills of central Wales? The answer must be that it was due to the unique combination of factors and features occurring in this area.

There is the range of habitats that attracted (and continues to attract) the bird to this area in the first place - the steep-sided valleys with hanging oakwoods clinging to their slopes, which are preferred nesting and roosting sites for the bird, and the high plateau of rolling open moorlands above the valleys, on which the kite hunts and feeds. These

Tregaron Bog

high sheepwalks are remote enough for a fair number of natural sheep casualties to occur, and this sheep carrion is an important part of the bird's diet.

Certainly the remoteness of the area has played a major part in enabling the kite to survive here. For there are scarcely any gamekeepers because of the low numbers of grouse, and few people, save the sheep farmers whose homes lie on the outer edges of the waste. This has allowed the red kite to avoid much of man's persecution, and here it has made its last stand, barely clinging to its existence until the conservationists, in 1903, began to stand up in the bird's defence.

To give you an idea of what the area must have been like in those early days of the kite's fight for survival, I have included here an extract describing the area as it were then.

The Reverend W. Williams in 1894 described the area thus:

> . . . there is a wild and mountainous tract of country lying between the counties of Brecon and Cardigan, where, for many miles in every direction, there are no human habitations, save here and there, in a deep dingle, just one house, the residence of the sheep-farmer, with three or four small cultivated fields in its immediate vicinity, and at some distance up the slopes of the mountains an occasional shepherd's hut. Crossing the range there is a bridle road leading from Llanwrtyd Wells, in the valley of the Irvon, to Tregaron, in the valley of the Teivi - a distance of about eighteen miles "as the crow flies", but of considerably more as the rider must travel. It is a magnificent ride, through scenery of the wildest grandeur. From the

highest points in his progress the traveller will descry nothing but a sea of mountains, some rounded, and some rugged and precipitous, extending in every direction - bluff after bluff, and precipice beyond precipice, and, as it seems to him, interminable. Here are the "Wolves' Leaps", where the Irvon, before it has become a river, has worn its rocky channel to an enormous depth, and rushes and gurgles in the dark caverns and recesses beneath, while the rocks on the surface on both sides nearly touch each other. Here, too, are the "Cock's paces", where the Towy, many miles before reaching the plain, does the same thing on a greater and grander scale. Here, likewise, near the spot where the Dothia and the Towy rush, with a deafening roar, into one another's embrace, and more than half way up a rugged and rocky cone, is "Twm Shon Catti's Cave", from whence, a couple of centuries ago, that celebrated outlaw was wont to issue forth, to spread terror and rapine through the surrounding districts. It is not a mountain at all that one traverses here, but a country of mountains. It is a path that a stranger would better not attempt alone, for the chances are that he would soon find his way into some place from which it would be exceedingly difficult to find his way out, and he might shout until he could do so no longer without making himself heard by any human being . . . [1]

Unfortunately, today some of the land has disappeared under conifer plantations and reservoirs, but much still remains as it was then in wild and glorious solitude where the red kite is being given the chance to breed and hopefully to flourish once again.

Underside of the Red Kite

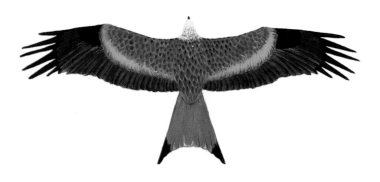

Upper points of the Red Kite

3. The Red Kite - *Milvus milvus*

Identification

The red kite, known in Welsh as *barcud*, is a bird with which there should be no real problems of identification in this country. It can be easily distinguished from other birds on account of its long and markedly forked tail, while the conspicuous white areas near the tips of the under-wing and the whitish head and throat, combined with the mainly rufous plumage, help to make the identification complete.

Even at a distance the notably cruciform silhouette and effortless flight are most distinctive. Its size varies from 60 – 66 cm (tail 28 – 32 cm) with a wing span from 175 – 195 cm.

Behaviour

The red kite is essentially a solitary raptor, never as gregarious as its relative the black kite, although small parties may be seen at food concentrations or scavenging points, a practice most often seen in winter.

Much of the bird's time is spent on the wing, and it is one of the most accomplished of all fliers. This buoyant and effortless flight was undoubtedly the reason why the child's flying toy was so named.

What a privilege it is to watch the bird as it circles over hillside or plain. It rises in the air in spirals on its motionless wings, sometimes tilting its body or adjusting its tail to gain maximum advantage of the thermals on which it rises. It is on these warm still days that one should look for the bird as the climatic conditions are then the most favourable for it to show off its majestic soaring and flying to the full. Sometimes on such days, if one is lucky, it is possible to see kite, buzzard, gull and crow, all effortlessly circling and rising on the same thermal together.

A good pair of binoculars is a must for watching the red kite,[1] as it often reaches such heights that it appears a mere speck in the sky. The binoculars will help both to identify the bird and follow it in its pursuits.

Habitat
The kite's preferred habitat is the open deciduous woodland in unpopulated upland valleys, which are used for nesting and roosting, and the high ground above the valleys of remote moorlands and rough grassland on which it hunts.

Nesting
Red kites build their nests in trees and there is no record of their using cliff ledges or crags. Their nests are bulky constructions of dead twigs, lined with sheep's wool. Often bits of paper, plastic and even rags are added to the nest, hence Shakespeare's warning in *The Winter's Tale*, "when the kite builds, look to lesser linen".[2]

Sometimes they will use old nests of buzzards or ravens. If breeding has been successful the bird will often return to the same nest year after year. One nest in Wales was used for 17 consecutive years.

Breeding

The red kite's eggs are white with red-brown blotches and are laid during the months of April and May. It lays a clutch of two usually but sometimes one or three. The incubation period is of 28 − 30 days and the young ones leave the nest when they are about 50 − 55 days old.

In this century the red kite has not been a particularly successful breeder. This is probably due to a number of reasons such as bad weather (the kite often lays its eggs early so they may be exposed to frost), the ravages of a severe winter with resultant food shortages, predation by such species as crows, squirrels etc., and of course the all too common theft of eggs or young.

Voice

The red kite's call is a shrill mewing 'wee-oo', higher pitched, weaker and more rapidly repeated than that of the buzzard; but it is used far less frequently.

Feeding

The bird hunts by soaring and circling over open ground often at considerable height, but sometimes by gliding low or even hovering over the ground.

The red kite eats a wide range of food items, being both predator and scavenger. Its diet consists in the main of small mammals (rabbits, voles, mice etc.), birds (especially young and injured), sheep carrion, some reptiles (mainly lizards and snakes), and occasionally fish. The kite will also scavenge for waste from slaughter houses and rubbish tips (the bird is frequently sighted at the rubbish dumps of a number of towns in the area).

Pen-y-garreg Reservoir, Elan Valley

Migration
Most kites are resident, often spending their winters in and around their home range, although some (mainly juveniles) make their way east into England or south down to Devon and Cornwall to winter.

Status and distribution
There is a small relict population confined to the remote hill country of central Wales of about 47 pairs, which in 1988 reared a total of 38 young.

4. Field Observation

Often the first indication of the presence of the red kite is the cawing note of the crows, who have taken wing to show their displeasure at the passing bird. The kite, like all other birds of prey, is frequently mobbed by other birds. These birds, most commonly crows (although I have seen buzzards mobbing the larger kite), will swoop and dive at the passing raptor, showing little regard for their own safety and will often pursue the bird long after it seems reasonable to do so. Many times I have been grateful to the crows, with their vociferous displays of aggression, for alerting me to the presence of a kite, for the bird uses its voice most sparingly, and unless in my direct field of view, no doubt the bird would have passed by unnoticed. I have read of someone who was watching kites on the continent, remarking that the birds there may have been completely silent.[1]

Once aware of its presence however the kite is unmistakable, wheeling in the sky, with its long wings bent at the wrist and its deeply forked chestnut tail, it makes other birds look almost cumbersome by comparison. In my youth, before I had seen the bird, other than in photographs, I would often ponder whether the buzzard I had just sighted may have been a kite and it was not until I had seen the bird myself, did I realise what a marked difference there is between the two birds and how much of my earlier confusion was down to wishful thinking.

I have often noticed how well the kite deals with strong winds, using its tail like a rudder and widely parting the finger-like tips of its wings, to give it a surprising amount of manoeuvrability in such bad conditions. However, during prolonged bad weather, the bird may stay at roost for much of the day, and as already stated, it is on the warm, still days that it is best to look for the kite as this is when it really comes into its own, completing its manoeuvres with absolute mastery of the air currents and thermals. Although most aerial activity consists of effortless high circling and soaring, I have sometimes observed that the kite will hunt 'harrier-like', with slow flapping wings or even hovering, low over the ground.

Upper Tyni Valley

The kite seems to be most active in the early morning or early evening with nest-building or hunting often occurring at such times. The bird's activities are carried out quite solitarily, but occasionally (especially in early spring), I have witnessed flocks of birds indulging in mutual soaring, sometimes even engaging in a mild form of flight-play. This high circling by flocks, could possibly be a part of a mating display leading to pair formation.

Very close views of the kite are hard to achieve, and it must be remembered that all observations should be inhibited by the need to leave the bird as undisturbed as possible in its nesting territories, for only by leaving the few mating pairs completely undisturbed can there be any chance of their survival. Of course this rule applies to all endangered species, but with the kite, I would suggest even more so. It seems to be among the shiest of all birds in and around its breeding areas. When disturbed by man, it slips away with little or no demonstration, and it has often been noted that the kite will desert its nest after the slightest of intrusions into its privacy. This shyness probably accounts for the fact that the bird, with its obvious preference to secure nesting sites, will if successful in breeding, return to the same nest for many years running.

Whilst watching the kite, I have found myself in many unusual and interesting situations. One would never consider, in order to watch such a rare and beautiful bird, a day could be spent at a rubbish tip. Recently, I spent a day at the Welsh Hawking Centre in Barry, after a television news report that a pair of kites were nesting in the trees near there, and were soon to be laying their eggs (I dread to think what might have happened to the birds if the story had been true, especially after witnessing the crowds who turned out to see the birds the next day). As I had suspected, the story turned out to be part truth, part speculation. There was a pair of kites there but they certainly were not nesting and there was little likelihood of them doing so, as the habitat there was totally unsuitable for breeding kites. The birds were in fact just a part of what has been termed the 'red kite explosion',[2] a massive influx of kites into this country in late March and early April, with sightings in London, Suffolk, Norfolk, Devon, Northumbria, the Shetlands, Orkney and Fair Isle. The reason why the birds turned up here in such numbers is not yet clearly established, but it seems that a combination of the weather conditions and the fact that the kites on the continent had a particularly good breeding season, would be the most likely explanation. The two birds at Barry which were a part of that invasion, probably decided to stay in the area to take advantage of a ready supply of food there, which had been left out for buzzards released back into the wild. Presumably like most of the birds that turned up in the country, they drifted back to the continent, but one would hope that these and some of the other birds managed to make contact with the resident Welsh population and decided to stay.

5. Where To Go To See the Red Kite

Whenever the kite population has been at its lowest, the birds have always been concentrated in the remote woodlands of the upper Tywi valley, and whenever there has been an increase in the population (as now) the distribution then extends to other parts of Wales.

As can be seen, I have included a map of central Wales, which shows the main areas today of the kites' distribution. I have also written some brief notes on these areas, which I hope will help in both locating the bird, and discovering some of the many places of interest in this most attractive part of Wales.

The method I would recommend for looking for the red kite, is to travel the area by car (it's certainly warmer and more comfortable that way), scanning the sky frequently and stopping at certain vantage points along the way. Another advantage of travelling by car, is that the kite, like most birds, appears at times not to connect a car with the human driving it, thus enabling many close observations of the bird through a carefully positioned car window. Though more often than not, the kite will be observed at a distance, and as pointed out previously a good pair of binoculars (or telescope) is a must for watching the bird.

A word of warning, one should never encroach on the bird in the woodlands in which it nests, for though the kite can at times be seen in the most unlikely places (rubbish tips etc.) without seeming to pay too much attention to the presence of man, in its breeding range it is notoriously susceptible to disturbance. I may add that walking in woodlands restricts the chances of seeing the bird as the range of visibility will be restricted by the trees.

Remember, it is not only in the summer months that one may see the red kite. As it is, by and large, a resident bird, there are chances of sighting it throughout the year. Actually these opportunities increase during the winter months, as this is when the birds often congregrate in groups, sometimes even scavenging in and around the towns in the area.

Llandovery

This bustling historic market town, once described by George Burrow in his book *Wild Wales*, as "about the pleasantest little town in which I have halted in the course of my wanderings", is a good base for exploring the spectacular countryside of the upper Tywi valley and its tributaries.

Nearby at Pant-y-celyn, is the home of the eighteenth-century Methodist hymn writer and preacher William Williams, author of *Guide me, O Thou great Jehovah (Bread of heaven)*.

Dinas Reserve (RSPB)

This is approximately 10 miles north of Llandovery, on an unclassified road to Llyn Brianne.

The Dinas is a steeply wooded conical hill, at the junction of the Doethie and Tywi valleys. Thirty years ago this was one of the last known nesting sites of the red kite, and although no longer nesting on the reserve, the bird is frequently sighted over the surrounding valleys. According to legend, the

Dinas was also once the home of Twm Sion Cati (a sort of Welsh Robin Hood) who reputedly lived here for some time in a cave.

A nature trail of 1½ miles runs around the foot of the hill (from which the cave may be reached by a short climb). The trail is open all year to visitors and an information centre at the reserve is open and manned between Easter and August.

Other birds seen on the reserve include peregrine, buzzard, sparrow hawk and raven.

Gwenffrwd Reserve (RSPB)

This is 10 miles north of Llandovery, on an unclassified road off the A40 driving via Cilycwm.

The 1100 acres of the reserve offer a range of habitat, including hanging oakwoods and moorlands rising to 1143 feet. There is a nature trail on the

Pant-y-celyn, home of William Williams

Llandovery

reserve, which is a walk of about four miles in all, and involves a climb on a fairly steady gradient from about 700 - 1100 feet.

Access to the reserve is strictly controlled from the Dinas information centre, and intending visitors should report there between 1000 and 1700 hours. The reserve is open from Easter to August on all days except Fridays.

Red kite, peregrine, red grouse and many other species of bird are resident on the reserve.

Llyn Brianne

Approximately 12 miles north of Llandovery, this spectacular man-made lake is situated right in the heart of the kite country. There is an elevated viewing platform which gives good views of the dam, while a new road running along the eastern side of

Sessile Oak Woods, Dinas Bird Reserve

the lake (which links up with the Llanwrtyd Wells - Abergwesyn - Tregaron mountain road) gives spectacular views of the lake and surrounding hill country.

Llanwrtyd Wells

This attractive little town was popular in Victorian times for its spa and wells, which were thought to cure a wide range of ailments. Now the town is earning a reputation as an outdoor activity resort, with trekking, riding, walking and fishing in the area.

Irfon valley

The unclassified mountain road, running from Llanwrtyd Wells to the tiny hamlet of Abergwesyn, offers some magnificent views of this beautiful river valley. There are two reserves in the area, the British National Trust's reserve of Craig Irfon and the Nature Conservancy Council's reserve of Nant Irfon. The whole of the area is one of steep valley sides, rock outcrops, cliffs, stands of conifers and the remains of the once extensive oakwoods. There are several picnic sites in the area, which offer good points for observation.

Red kite, peregrine, merlin and all the other representative high ground birds are seen here.

Abergweswyn - Tregaron mountain road

This road, once used by cattle drovers journeying to London and the Midlands, travels through some of the most lonely and remote scenery in Wales. The road is unfenced, and there are several good pull-off points along the way.

Llanwrtyd Church

Llanwrtyd Wells

Tregaron

This is a small market town, in and around which the kite is frequently sighted.

A major attraction to the bird in this area (especially in winter) is the nearby Tregaron bog, (Cors Caron) which is host to many species of bird, including red kite, hen harrier, merlin and buzzard.

The best views of the bog are obtained from the B434 road which runs north east from Tregaron, following the eastern boundary of the bog. There is limited parking just off the road.

Whilst in the area, one may also like to visit the nearby abbey ruins of Strata Florida (Ystrad Fflur). The abbey, which was built in 1164, was once the "Westminster Abbey of Wales".

Wye - Elan woods

Near where the river Elan joins the river Wye, south of the attractive country town of Rhayader, are the four small areas of land owned by the RSPB; comprising three woodland areas, Dyffryn (54 acres), Cwm (18 acres), Glanllyn (100 acres) and the high plateau of Carn Gafallt (643 acres).

This area is particularly rich in woodland birds, and at least eight species of raptor have been seen here, including the red kite, peregrine and sparrow hawk.

The areas of Dyffryn wood, and Carn Gaffallt are open to the public at all times.

Elan valley reservoirs

Here in a wild, remote stretch of the Cambrian mountains are the five Elan valley reservoirs, Craig Goch, Penygarreg, Garreg-ddu, Caban-Coch

The Talbot Hotel, Tregaron

Strata Florida

Elan Valley

Hafod Arms, Devil's Bridge

and Claerwen. All five reservoirs can be easily viewed from the public roads in the area.

These lonely uplands offer some spectacular scenery, and red kites and many other birds of the high ground are seen in the area.

Rhayader - Cwm Ystwyth mountain road
This is a mountain road which travels through the typical high ground hunting areas of the red kite.

The Rheidol valley
Probably one of the best ways to explore this area is to take one of the "Great Little Trains of Wales", which run the 12 miles between the sea resort and university town of Aberystwyth and Devil's Bridge. The line was built in 1902, to carry ore from the lead mines around Devil's Bridge. The train runs from Easter to mid September.

Alternatively, if you travel by road, an unclassified road leaves the A44 at Capel Bangor and follows the whole valley; or the A4120, which runs east from Aberystwyth on the high ground at the south of the valley, offers breathtaking views of the whole area.

Visitors to Devil's Bridge are well advised to take the steep footpath, to witness for themselves the spectacular falls and scenery surrounding the bridges there.

The red kite is resident in the area, as well as many other species of woodland birds.

Ponterwyd - Talybont mountain road
This road, which travels through the lonely hills and countryside, was once travelled by that much

celebrated author George Borrow (whose book written in 1854, describing his travels throughout Wales, is still available in shops today).

Although today some of the area is covered by the Nant-Y-Moch and Rheidol lakes, much remains as wild and remote as it was then.

The inn at Ponterwyd, where George Borrow spent the night after wandering in the hills, is now named after him in his honour.

The red kite is often seen hunting in this area, and there are many picnic sites along the road, which offer good vantage points to survey the area.

George Borrow Hotel

Machynthleth

Machynlleth

This is the town where, in 1404, Owain Glyndŵr presided over his "Parliament of Wales".

Today, the town is the main shopping and touring centre of the lower Dovey valley and the building where the parliament once sat is now an information centre with historic exhibitions.

Visitors to the town may also like to visit the nearby Centre for Alternative Technology, which is open daily to the public.

Machynlleth - Llanidloes mountain road

This road, which travels through some beautiful scenery, will take you past the six mile long Clywedog reservoir, and there are many lay-bys on the road skirting the lake which give wonderful views of the area.

Llanddewi Brefi

This is a small village nestling deep in the undisturbed uplands of mid Wales. The village is dominated by a church, built on the mound which according to legend rose under the feet of St David as he preached.

Lampeter

This is the "capital" of the upper Teifi valley and a busy town which is the centre of farming life in the area.

It is also the home of one of the colleges of the University of Wales, which is open to visitors.

Pumsaint

Near the small village of Pumsaint are the old Roman gold mines of Dolaucothi, now owned by the National

Trust. These gold mines, set amid the wooded hill-sides overlooking the beautiful Cothi Valley, were the only site in Britain where the Romans mined for gold.

Visitors can be taken on an underground tour of the mines, if they wish. The mines are open from Easter to October. During mid-summer only, there are underground tours.

Llanidloes

This small market town at the junction of the Severn and Clywedog rivers, is ideally situated as a touring centre for those wishing to explore the Clywedog reservoir and surrounding countryside. The town's most striking feature is the sixteenth-century market hall which stands on timbers above the open market place.

The upper floor of the building is now a local museum which is open to visitors.

Llanwrthwl

This is a pleasant little village on the banks of the River Wye. Good fishing for both trout and salmon is available here.

Just off the A470, a few miles south of the village, is a motel, touring caravan park and restaurant.

Rhandirmwyn

Set on a hillside overlooking the wild and beautiful upper Tywi valley, this picturesque village was once important for the lead that was mined in the area.

There are many farmhouses in the area, which offer accommodation and the chance to sample some traditional home-made cooking.

Market Hall, Llanidloes

Lampeter College

Notes and References

Chapter One

1. Bannerman, D.A. and Lodge, G.E. (1956). *Birds of the British Isles*, Vol. V, Oliver and Boyd, p. 260.
2. *ibid.*, p. 261.
3. *ibid.*
4. Shakespeare, W., *Coriolanus*, Act IV, Scene V, l. 42.
5. Although not found in Britain other than as a rare vagrant, the black kite (*Milvus migrans*) is a well known scavenger in many parts of the world. This scavenging is often carried out with a remarkable degree of boldness and ingenuity, indeed my father has often recounted to me the story of how, when he was stationed in the Middle East during the Second World War, the black kites would swoop down and snatch the food off the plates of any unwary soldier leaving the mess tent.
6. Bannerman, D.A. and Lodge, G.E., *op. cit.*, p. 261.
7. *ibid.*, p. 262.
8. Today the fund is administered by the Kite Committee, a group of people from many of the organizations for conservation, who work together to ensure the protection and further development of the red kite in this country.

Chapter Two

1. Bannerman, D.A and Lodge, G.E. *op. cit.*, p. 270.
2. *Bird Watching*, June (1988), p. 53.

Chapter Three

1. Don't go in for the so-called "high magnification" binoculars (15x, 20x, etc.) for not only are they usually of a poor optical quality, but also their very restricted field of view and their sheer weight and size make it difficult for the user to keep them trained onto a bird, especially when in flight. Better to stick to 7x, 8x or 10x magnification. The Zeiss 10 x 40B, although expensive, are ideal for watching raptors.
2. Shakespeare, W., *The Winter's Tale*, Act IV, Scene III, l. 23-24.

Chapter Four

1. Williams, Rev. W., Second Edition (1884), *Welsh Calvinistic Methodism*, p. 152.

Bibliography

Bannerman, D.A. and Lodge, G.E. (1956). *Birds of the British Isles*, Vol. V. Oliver and Boyd.

Condry, W.M. (1981). *The Natural History of Wales*. New Naturalist Series.

Cramp, S. and Simmons, K.E.L. (eds) (1980). *Handbook of the Birds of Europe, the Middle East, and North Africa: The Birds of the Western Palearctic*, Vol. II. Oxford University Press.

Fisher, J. (1948). *The Natural History of the Red Kite*. RSPB.

Hammond, N. (ed.) (1983). *RSPB Nature Reserves*. RSPB.

Hywel-Davies, J. and Thom, V. (eds) (1984). *Guide to Britain's Nature Reserves*. Macmillan.

Lockley, R.M. (1970). *The Naturalist in Wales*. David and Charles.

Saunders, D. (1987). *Where to Watch Birds in Wales*. Christopher Helm.

List of Illustrations